COOKING CHEMISTRY
HOW DOES CHEESE CURDLE?

by Tracy Vonder Brink

pogo

Ideas for Parents and Teachers

Pogo Books let children practice reading informational text while introducing them to nonfiction features such as headings, labels, sidebars, maps, and diagrams, as well as a table of contents, glossary, and index.

Carefully leveled text with a strong photo match offers early fluent readers the support they need to succeed.

Before Reading

- "Walk" through the book and point out the various nonfiction features. Ask the student what purpose each feature serves.
- Look at the glossary together. Read and discuss the words.

During Reading

- Have the child read the book independently.
- Invite them to list questions that arise from reading.

After Reading

- Discuss the child's questions. Talk about how they might find answers to those questions.
- Prompt the child to think more. Ask: Have you ever thought about how cheese is made? What other questions do you have about cheese?

Pogo Books are published by Jump!
3500 American Blvd W, Suite 150
Bloomington, MN 55431
www.jumplibrary.com

Copyright © 2026 Jump!
International copyright reserved in all countries. No part of this book may be reproduced in any form without written permission from the publisher.

Jump! is a division of FlutterBee Education Group.

Library of Congress Cataloging-in-Publication Data

Names: Vonder Brink, Tracy, author.
Title: How does cheese curdle? / by Tracy Vonder Brink.
Description: Minneapolis, MN: Jump!, Inc., [2026]
Series: Cooking chemistry | Includes index.
Audience: Ages 7-10
Identifiers: LCCN 2025000585 (print)
LCCN 2025000586 (ebook)
ISBN 9798892138345 (hardcover)
ISBN 9798892138352 (paperback)
ISBN 9798892138369 (ebook)
Subjects: LCSH: Cheesemaking–Juvenile literature. Cheese–Juvenile literature.
Milk–Curdling–Juvenile literature.
Classification: LCC SF271 .V659 2026 (print)
LCC SF271 (ebook)
DDC 637/.3–dc23/eng/20250219
LC record available at https://lccn.loc.gov/2025000585
LC ebook record available at https://lccn.loc.gov/2025000586

Editor: Katie Chanez
Designer: Anna Peterson

Photo Credits: SergeyZavalnyuk/iStock, cover; Sastom007/Shutterstock, 1; Mix Tape/Shutterstock, 3; Olgysha/Shutterstock, 4; Rafa Jodar/iStock, 5 (foreground); Aleksey Gromov/iStock, 5 (background); Lysenko Andrii/Shutterstock, 6; Esperanza33/iStock, 7; Oleksandr Yakoniuk/Shutterstock, 8-9; RESTOCK images/Shutterstock, 10; Artemidovna/iStock, 10-11 (cheese); SlayStorm/iStock, 10-11 (pepper); wanderluster/iStock, 12-13; CasarsaGuru/iStock, 14-15; JGA/Shutterstock, 16-17; Diane Labombarbe/iStock, 18 (recipe card); Tanya Sid/Shutterstock, 18 (salt); AlenKadr/Shutterstock, 18 (lemon juice); Artiom Photo/Shutterstock, 18 (milk); Katie Chanez, 19-21; Africa Studio/Shutterstock, 23.

Printed in the United States of America at Corporate Graphics in North Mankato, Minnesota.

TABLE OF CONTENTS

CHAPTER 1
Made from Milk 4

CHAPTER 2
Cheese Science 6

CHAPTER 3
Let's Make Cheese! 18

ACTIVITIES & TOOLS
Try This! 22
Glossary 23
Index 24
To Learn More 24

CHAPTER 1

MADE FROM MILK

There are many kinds of cheeses. Some are hard and crumbly. Others are soft and creamy. Each kind tastes different.

The main **ingredient** in cheese is milk. Cow milk is used most often. Some cheeses are made with milk from other animals. Goat milk, sheep milk, and even moose milk can become cheese!

CHAPTER 1 | 5

CHAPTER 2
CHEESE SCIENCE

Milk is sent to a **creamery**. Starter is added to the milk. Starters are made of good **bacteria**. Different starters are used to make different cheeses.

starter

Milk has fat, **proteins**, sugars, and water. Starter changes the milk's sugars into **acid**. The acid makes the milk curdle, or separate into clumps.

CHAPTER 2

Rennet is also added. It helps the proteins stick together. This makes them solid. The solid clumps are called curds. The leftover liquid is called whey.

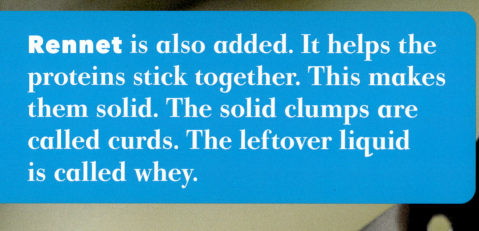

curd

whey

CHAPTER 2

TAKE A LOOK!

Rennet helps curdle milk. How? Take a look!

1 Milk proteins and fat float in water.

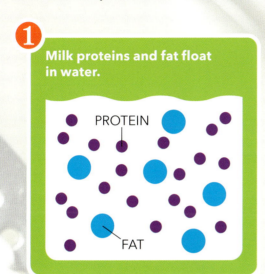

2 Each protein clump has hairlike parts. They keep the clumps from sticking together.

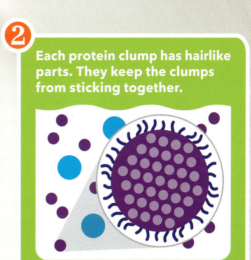

3 Rennet takes off the hairlike parts.

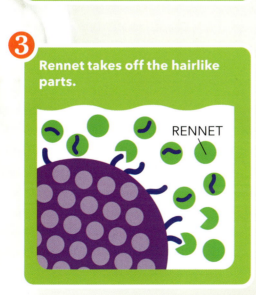

4 The proteins stick together. Curds form.

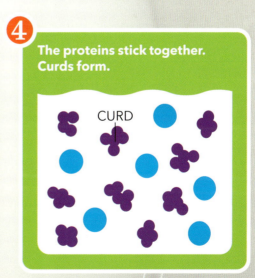

CHAPTER 2

A cheesemaker takes the curds out of the whey. They **add salt and other ingredients** to the curds. For example, peppers are added to make pepper jack cheese.

DID YOU KNOW?

Cheesemakers sometimes add **mold** to curds! The mold is safe to eat. It changes the **flavor**. The mold gives the cheese blue spots. Because of this, it is called blue cheese.

blue cheese

CHAPTER 2

The curds go into a cheese mold. A mold gives a cheese its shape. Some are round. Others are rectangular.

CHAPTER 2 13

A machine presses the mold. This squeezes out more whey. It also makes the cheese **firm**.

DID YOU KNOW?

Whey has a lot of protein. Leftover whey is often used to make protein bars and powders.

14 CHAPTER 2

Some cheeses are **aged** after they are pressed. The bacteria break down sugars in the cheese. This makes the flavor stronger. Cheeses may age for weeks. Some age for years! Then the cheeses are ready to enjoy!

DID YOU KNOW?

Cottage cheese and cream cheese are soft cheeses. They are not pressed or aged. They are made with acid. They often do not have rennet.

CHAPTER 2

CHAPTER 3

LET'S MAKE CHEESE!

Cottage cheese can be made with an acid like lemon juice. You can make it! All you need are three ingredients and an adult's help. Let's try!

COTTAGE CHEESE

INGREDIENTS
½ gallon (1.9 liters) of whole milk
lemon juice
salt

KITCHEN TOOLS
large pot
spoon
mesh strainer or colander with a cheesecloth
2 bowls

START WITH THESE STEPS:

1

Pour the milk into a large pot.

2

Have an adult heat the milk. Cook until bubbles form.

CHAPTER 3 | 19

3

Stir the milk. Slowly add lemon juice one tablespoon (15 milliliters) at a time. Keep stirring. Stop adding lemon juice when the milk starts to clump. Stir for three to four more minutes.

4

Have an adult pour the milk mixture through a strainer or colander with a cheesecloth over a bowl. This will catch the curds.

5

Gently press the curds with a spoon to squeeze out the rest of the liquid.

6

Put the curds in a bowl. Add a pinch of salt. Let the cottage cheese cool. Enjoy!

CHAPTER 3 21

ACTIVITIES & TOOLS

TRY THIS!

MAKE YOUR OWN CHEESE

Vinegar is an acid. It can be used to make cheese. Try making soft, crumbly cheese with this fun activity!

What You Need:
- ½ gallon (1.9 L) of whole milk
- ¼ cup (60 mL) of white vinegar
- salt
- large pot
- spoon
- baking thermometer
- cheesecloth or other thin fabric
- mesh strainer or colander
- bowl
- plastic wrap

1. Pour the milk in a large pot.
2. Have an adult heat the milk on a stovetop until it reaches 195 degrees Fahrenheit (90 degrees Celsius). Stir constantly.
3. Add the vinegar. Stir for 30 seconds. Then let it sit for 10 minutes.
4. Add a pinch of salt.
5. Put the cheesecloth or other thin fabric into the strainer or colander. Place the strainer or colander over a bowl. Pour the milk mixture into it. Let it strain for one hour.
6. Pat the cheese into a ball. Wrap it in plastic wrap and place it in the fridge until it is chilled.

GLOSSARY

acid: A substance with a sour taste that reacts to a base to form a salt.

aged: Set aside for a period of time.

bacteria: Microscopic, single-celled living things that exist everywhere.

creamery: A place where butter and cheese are made.

firm: Solid.

flavor: Taste.

ingredient: An item used to make something.

mold: A fungus that grows on food or things that are warm and moist.

proteins: Nutrients that are found in all living things and are necessary for life.

rennet: A substance found in the stomach of animals that is used to make cheese.

ACTIVITIES & TOOLS 23

INDEX

acid 7, 17, 18
aged 17
animals 5
bacteria 6, 17
cheesemaker 10
cheese mold 13, 14
creamery 6
curds 8, 9, 10, 13, 20, 21
fat 7, 9
ingredient 5, 10, 18

milk 5, 6, 7, 9, 18, 19, 20
mold 10
proteins 7, 8, 9, 14
rennet 8, 9, 17
salt 10, 18, 21
soft cheeses 4, 17
starter 6, 7
sugars 7, 17
water 7, 9
whey 8, 10, 14

TO LEARN MORE

Finding more information is as easy as 1, 2, 3.
1. Go to www.factsurfer.com
2. Enter "cheese" into the search box.
3. Choose your book to see a list of websites.